THE PEARL

NOTES

including
- *Life and Background of the Author*
- *An Introduction to* The Pearl
- *List of Characters*
- *Chapter Summaries and Critical Commentaries*
- *Characters and Characterization*
- *The Source for Steinbeck's* The Pearl
- *The Legend of "The Pearl of the World"*
- The Pearl: *A Critical Approach*
- *Questions and Discussion Topics*
- *Selected Bibliography*

by
Eva Fitzwater, Ph.D.
Midland College

Wiley Publishing, Inc.

Editor
Gary Carey, M.A., University of Colorado

Consulting Editor
James L. Roberts, Ph.D., Department of
English, University of Nebraska

Publisher's Acknowledgments
Acquisitions Editor: Greg Tubach
Glossary Editors: The editors and staff at
Webster's New World Dictionaries
Editorial Assistant: Meagan Burger
Composition
Wiley Publishing, Inc., Indianapolis Composition
Services

CliffsNotes™ *The Pearl*

Published by:
Wiley Publishing, Inc.
111 River Street
Hoboken, NJ 07030
www.wiley.com

Copyright © 1981 Wiley Publishing, Inc., New York, New York
Library of Congress Control Number is available from the publisher.
ISBN: 0-8220-0994-3

15 14 13 12 11

Published by Wiley Publishing, Inc., New York, NY
Published simultaneously in Canada

For general information on our other products and services or to obtain technical support, please contact our Customer
Care Department within the U.S. at 800-762-2974, outside the U.S. at 317-572-3993, or fax 317-572-4002.

Wiley also publishes its books in a variety of electronic formats. Some content that appears in print may not be available in electronic books.

CONTENTS

THE PEARL NOTES

LIFE AND BACKGROUND OF THE AUTHOR

John Steinbeck was the type of author who liked to know his material firsthand. He was not content to narrate a story which had no basis in fact. Thus, many of his works take place in California, where he lived, and they deal with subjects which he thoroughly understood. Within his novels are characters who seem to breathe the very reality of life itself. When not writing about his native California and its citizens, he would use people whom he had become intimate with in other ways (see discussion of *The Grapes of Wrath* below). *The Pearl* was based on real characters whom Steinbeck became acquainted with during one of his prolonged travels, as also noted below. Consequently, one of the finest attributes of *The Pearl* is the feeling that the author knows his material and his characters in great depth and with perfect accuracy. The scenes in this novel, from its opening with the primitive pearl fishers to the corruptness of the town, are narrated with the skill of a person who has witnessed the events.

Steinbeck's father settled in California shortly after the American Civil War. John Steinbeck was born in Salinas on February 27, 1902. His mother was a schoolteacher in the public school system of Salinas. Steinbeck grew up in this beautiful, fertile California valley, where he found the material for most of his novels. His imagination was kindled by writing at a very early age partly because his mother, the schoolteacher, read to him from the famous literature of the world.

During his formative years, he played various sports in high school, worked at many different jobs, and wandered around the countryside observing the phenomena of nature. He entered Stanford University in 1920, and even though he remained until 1925, he never graduated. In fact, he earned very few college credits. He did, however, contribute some poems and short stories to the Stanford literary magazine.

During his years at Stanford and immediately after his departure, Steinbeck worked at a variety of jobs. He went to New York in 1925, but found it unsuitable to his temperament. He returned to California and between odd jobs, he began writing his novels. His first novel, *Cup of Gold*, appeared in 1929.

In two respects, 1930 was a notable year for Steinbeck. He married Carol Henning and the newlyweds settled in staid Pacific Grove, which he sometimes satirized in his writings. There, Steinbeck met Ed Ricketts, whose friendship strongly influenced Steinbeck's work. Ricketts was the owner of a biological supply laboratory on Monterey's Cannery Row, and Steinbeck's novel *Cannery Row* is dedicated to "Ed Ricketts, *who knows why or should.*" In relationship to *The Pearl*, Ricketts' influence was tremendous. In the late thirties, Steinbeck and Ricketts became partners and engaged in a lengthy exploration of marine life along the shores of the Gulf of the California Baja, the setting of *The Pearl*. It was here that Steinbeck met the type of Indians who became the characters in *The Pearl*, and it was here that he first heard the story of the "pearl of great price." In another book, written as a description of this trip, *The Sea of Cortez*, Steinbeck describes the simple humanity of these native people in their struggle against nature and in their attempt to give a sense of dignity to their lives as they are being constantly cheated by forces in society which they cannot comprehend. As a result of his trip with Ed Ricketts, Steinbeck writes of these people in *The Pearl* with complete conviction.

By 1935, with the publication of *Tortilla Flat*, Steinbeck was now being recognized as an important American writer. *Tortilla Flat* was awarded the Gold Medal of the Commonwealth Club of San Francisco as the year's best novel by a Californian, even though critics missed the point of the droll humor about the unemployed drifters of Monterey. Steinbeck received between three and four thousand dollars for the Hollywood film rights.

During 1935, Steinbeck tried writing in Mexico but he returned to Los Gatos, California. *In Dubious Battle* (1936), concerned with a strike, aroused the critics' fury as Steinbeck had predicted. With a demand for his controversial work, he placed short stories in *Esquire* and *Harper's* and wrote a series of articles for the *San Francisco News* concerning life in California's migrant labor camps, material he used later for *The Grapes of Wrath*.

Of Mice and Men (1937), a popular and a critical success, was selected by the Book-of-the-Month Club, and shortly afterward Steinbeck was selected as one of the Ten Outstanding Young Men of the Year. After touring England and Ireland, Russia and Sweden, he produced a play version of the book with the famous playwright, George Kaufman. Steinbeck became a celebrity when the play enjoyed a long run, won the New York Drama Critics' Circle award on the first ballot and later became a popular film.

Unsurprisingly, however, the night that *Of Mice and Men* opened on Broadway, Steinbeck was living in a migrant camp. In preparation for writing his novels, Steinbeck would often live, work, and be with the people about whom he was to write. Thus, in preparation for writing *The Grapes of Wrath*, Steinbeck went to Oklahoma, joined some migrants and rode with them to California. Once in California, he stayed with the migrants, living with them in "Hoovervilles," joining them in their search for work, and attempting as nearly as possible to come to terms with their essential characteristics. Leaving them, he made several trips to various camps to observe firsthand the living and working conditions of migrants. He wrote some short pieces in which he described the plight of these people and pleaded for a more tolerant approach in dealing with them. These articles, however, were not very effective. It was only when he molded his new experiences into the form of a novel that positive effects were achieved.

The appearance of *The Grapes of Wrath* was the major publishing event of 1939. *Publishers Weekly* listed the novel as the best seller of 1939 and the eighth ranking book of 1940. It was estimated that over half a million copies of the original printing were sold. In addition to several American editions, there have been numerous foreign editions and translations. The novel later became a highly significant social protest film. Also in 1940, Steinbeck was elected to membership in the National Institute of Arts and Letters and won the Pulitzer Prize for having written the best novel of the year, as well as the American Booksellers' award.

In 1939 and 1940, Steinbeck set off with Ed Ricketts for expeditions to the Gulf of California, later documented in *The Sea of Cortez.* He also went to Mexico to film *The Forgotten Village,* a semidocumentary about introducing medicine into a suspicious community.

During 1942, Steinbeck's wife sued for divorce and that same year, the Army Air Force requested a promotional book, *Bombs Away*, to popularize the flight training program and to allay parental fears about flying. Steinbeck gave the royalties to the Air Forces Aid Society.

Steinbeck's World War II works included the play-novella, *The Moon Is Down*, for which he was decorated by the King of Norway in recognition of the book's contribution to the liberation effort. His film scenario *Lifeboat* is sometimes thought to be his most significant war writing. His human-interest articles, written while he was a special war correspondent for the New York *Herald Tribune* from June to December, 1943, appeared as a collection, *Once There Was a War*, in 1958. Evidently, Steinbeck had considered writing a novel about the war but in *The Wide World of John Steinbeck*, Peter Lisca comments that Steinbeck was "too disheartened by what he had seen of the war to prolong the experience in any way and he decided not to publish it."

After the war, Steinbeck devoted himself almost wholly to writing novels (*East of Eden* was made into a movie in 1956, starring the popular late actor James Dean and also Julie Harris, and in 1981, it was made into a critically acclaimed eight hour mini-series for television). Steinbeck's last major novel, *The Winter of Our Discontent*, appeared in 1961 and won high critical acclaim for its author. In 1962, Steinbeck was awarded the Nobel Prize for Literature, the highest honor a writer can receive. Of his many works, *The Pearl* has always been a favorite with readers of all ages. Steinbeck died in 1969.

AN INTRODUCTION TO *THE PEARL*: THE LEVELS OF MEANING

Even though *The Pearl* is outwardly a simple and beautiful book, there are several ways in which it can be read and appreciated. First, there is, as was just suggested, the beauty and power of the narrative itself. One need go no further than simply noting the power, the restraint, and the beauty with which Steinbeck narrates this simple story. The entire book rings with authenticity. As noted above, Steinbeck was thoroughly familiar with his material, and thus the novel, through its narrative and characterization, conveys a sense of the very essence of primitive life with all of its trials and rewards.

Second, some critics consider the novel from an ecological point of view. Just before writing this novel, John Steinbeck and his friend Ed Ricketts were exploring the seacoast in terms of the ecological functions of the various organisms that existed there. It was during this exploration that Steinbeck first heard of the story of the "Pearl of the World," a large pearl which was eventually tossed back into the sea from where it was originally taken. Because of Steinbeck's interest in ecology at the time, some critics have understandably viewed the novel as Steinbeck's statement about the need for the ecology to be left as undisturbed as possible. When one takes a great pearl from its natural setting, then one is destroying a part of the natural order of things, which could result in some type of disaster.

Third, there is the obvious sociological interpretation. In many of his previous novels, Steinbeck was interested in the relationship between the worker and capital. *In Dubious Battle* and *The Grapes of Wrath* both show the plight of the working man at the hands of unscrupulous and evil landowners. Also in this novel, we have a conflict between the simple and naive pearl fishers and the pearl buyers, who use their position to exploit the powerless natives. Likewise, there is the doctor and the priest who have shown no particular concern for the dreadful plight of the natives until there is the rumor about the Pearl of the World. Earlier, the doctor had selfishly and callously refused to treat Coyotito's scorpion bite because the child's father, Kino, had no money to pay. Likewise, the priest had used his church authority to teach the natives that they were to be content with their station in life because it blended with God's concept that everything has its own place in the world. Immediately upon hearing about the pearl, however, the priest begins to think about the repairs in the church that could be attended to with the price of the great pearl.

Then, too, there is the obvious level of the parable, or the allegorical or symbolic level of interpretation. The pearl is a pearl of great price. It represents the vanity of human wishes. With the pearl, Kino can do all the things that he has never dared to do before. But then, as Steinbeck writes in the introduction: "If this story is a parable, perhaps everyone takes his own meaning from it and reads his own life into it." Steinbeck's warning is especially true when we remember that since the Middle Ages, a pearl has been used in literature to represent spiritual purity and chastity, and the possession of a great pearl is a perfect symbol, then, to symbolize the goodness of the world. Yet, Steinbeck reverses this symbol here because his pearl represents evil, and only by casting it away can Kino regain a spiritual sense of well-being.

Philosophically, the novel is concerned with life and death and the meaning of both. During the course of the story, a simple family, through no particular fault, is brought to a tragic end. Their pearl is supposed to be used to bring their child out of darkness and into the world of light; he will be able to learn to read and write, and he will then be able to help all of the natives. Instead, the pearl becomes the direct instrument of the child's death.

In conclusion, while reading the novel one can find aspects of the story which will support any of the above interpretations. The greatness of this novel is that at any level, or at all of them, it is a beautiful tale told with wonderful precision and perfect simplicity.

LIST OF CHARACTERS

Kino

The young Indian pearl diver who finds the magnificent pearl and whose life is partially destroyed by this pearl.

Juana

Kino's wife and faithful partner in eking out a meager living; she is obedient and devoted to her family.

Coyotito

Coyotito is Kino and Juana's infant son; he is bitten by a scorpion and recovers miraculously only to be later killed by a bullet, a bullet intended for Kino.

Juan Tomás

Kino's brother, advisor, and his only protector when Kino is hunted for murder.

Apolonia

Juan's fat wife, who has no real significance in the story.

The Doctor

A thoroughly heartless, self-seeking man whose love of money is displayed when he refuses to help Coyotito because Kino cannot pay him his fee.

The Priest

The discovery of the pearl is said to "put a thoughtful look in his eyes and a memory of certain repairs necessary to the church."

The Pearl Buyers

They are unnamed in the story, and as a group, they represent the exploitation and hypocrisy that the Indians encounter.

SUMMARIES AND COMMENTARIES

CHAPTER ONE

Since Steinbeck will use the already established Indian legend of "The Pearl of the World" as a basis for his story, he begins the first chapter with events leading up to the discovery of the great pearl as recorded in Indian folklore (consult the section entitled "The Source for *The Pearl* and the 'Legend of the Pearl' "). In other words, the main legend begins with the discovery of the pearl and the effects that the discovery has on a young Indian boy. Steinbeck thus begins his novella by introducing us to the type of life that Kino lived *before* the discovery of the pearl so as to contrast the effects of the discovery on not only himself but also its effects on his entire family.

It is equally important to note that the novel opens at the dawn of a new day – a day that will bring, first, a disaster in the form of the scorpion and then, later in the day, the great discovery of the Pearl of the World. Then, Chapter Six closes the novel with the end of another day, its focus being three days later with the chastened and saddened Kino and Juana returning to the shores of the Gulf to throw the "evil" pearl back into the water.

As noted, Steinbeck begins his novel with a simple description of the natural surroundings. It is dawn and the beginning of a new day. Both Kino and his wife arise and go about their usual morning habits. His wife, Juana, prepares the fire, checks on the baby, Coyotito, and makes their meager breakfast while Kino sits and watches the ocean and remembers one of the ancient songs that come from his culture – the *Song of the Family*. It is a song from the old traditions of his race, and as he remembers the song, he takes pleasure in watching his wife go about her chores. He even watches some ants moving hastily about; in general, "it was a morning like other mornings and yet perfect among mornings."

The perfection of the morning, however, is about to be destroyed. After Kino has eaten the simple breakfast that he eats every morning – a hot corncake dipped in sauce – he suddenly becomes aware that a scorpion is slowly descending into the basket where the baby, Coyotito, is lying. As the scorpion moves down the rope of the hanging crib, Coyotito spots it and is excited by its movement. Juana immediately utters an ancient incantation from far back in her cultural past and also one *Hail Mary*. Kino inches quietly but steadily towards the scorpion, frightened to move too fast lest he cause the scorpion to sting. Other ancient songs come to his head – the *Song of Evil* is foremost in his thoughts. Without warning, the baby makes a sudden move, jarring the scorpion, and it falls into the basket and immediately stings Coyotito. In an extreme fit of primitive rage, Kino grabs the scorpion and rubs it "to a paste in his hands." Meanwhile, Juana grabs the baby and sucks as much of the poison out of the wound as is possible.

By this time the entire Indian village is aware of the situation, and everyone is thoroughly taken aback when Juana tells Kino to go for the doctor. Never in the memory of any of the Indians has the doctor ever come to attend any of them. The doctor will not come, and so Juana suddenly decides to take the dying child into town to the doctor. The entire village follows her. Along the way, others from the poorer section follow to see what will happen; even the beggars from in front of the church join in the procession because it is the beggars who best know the doctor. "They knew the doctor. They knew his ignorance, his cruelty, his avarice, his appetites, his sins. They knew his clumsy abortions and the little brown pennies he gave sparingly for alms."

Already in this procession, Steinbeck presents the town divided between two types—the old natives who have been a part of the country for centuries and the new Christian settlers, one of whom Kino and Juana are about to approach. Even as Kino and Juana reach the door of the doctor's house, Kino is filled with rage because he knows that "this doctor was not of his people. This doctor was of a race which for nearly four hundred years had beaten and starved and robbed and despised Kino's race." The doctor's servant will not even speak to Kino in Kino's native language, and he quickly closes the gate before going to inform the doctor of Kino's request for medical aid for Coyotito.

The doctor is a contrast to all the others: he is dressed in opulence and is lying in bed, sipping chocolate and dreaming of a past time when he lived in Paris. Upon hearing about Kino's request, he immediately sends the servant down to see if Kino can pay. Kino gives the servant his entire savings—a few "misshapen seed pearls, as ugly and gray as little ulcers." Quickly, the servant closes the gate, returns almost immediately with Kino's pearls, and tells him that the doctor is out. In angry frustration, Kino strikes his fist against the doctor's closed gates.

Throughout this first chapter, Steinbeck uses several techniques to emphasize the differences between the simple native Indians and the more cultured European types. For example, from the very beginning, there is some type of musical theme or composition running through Kino's mind. When he awakens, there is the *Song of the Family*. It is a song of security, warmth, and love. The novella opens on this song and it will later be replaced in the last chapters by the *Song of Evil*. The introduction of this basic song motif emphasizes the primitive reactions of these characters to life and to their surroundings. When these songs occur to a character, they will reflect part of that character's thoughts and feelings. When Kino hears Juana sing her morning song, he feels the warmth of her love and security: "Sometimes it rose to an aching chord that caught the throat, saying this is safety, this is warmth, this is the *whole*."

The *Song of the Family* is interrupted by the appearance of the deadly and dangerous scorpion, and then we hear the *Song of Evil*. The appearance of the scorpion threatens the security and safety of the family as a unit, and thus the *Song of Evil* prepares us for all the other evil that appears to destroy the family. The scorpion with its

poisonous sting is a foreshadowing of the human evil which will attack the family later.

There are several techniques of a basic nature used to suggest the
fundamental quality of the family. In the beginning, Kino awakens
in darkness, and the light gradually appears. Thus, the novella will
move in terms of various shades of light and dark. Steinbeck inten-
tionally chooses the most basic symbol because he is dealing with the
most basic and primitive emotions. Note that now there are various
mentions of light inside the house and the suggestions of the
darkness outside which reemphasize the *Song of the Family*. Gradually, then, the darkness on the outside diminishes as Kino prepares to
enter the world to undertake the support of his family.

The mixture of the old and the new is seen by the fact that Juana
prays for her stricken child by uttering an incantation of ancient
magic and then she says a *Hail Mary*. Consequently, the new has not
completely eradicated the old.

Steinbeck provides descriptions of the village and of the town,
both inside and outside the dwellings. These descriptions reiterate
the contrast between the old and the new worlds, and they suggest
that these two worlds can never blend into one unified group. Thus,
later the natives are suspicious of the pearl buyers because the
buyers represent the new world and are not to be trusted. Physically,
this contrast is illustrated by the dividing line between the city and
the brush town. When Juana is taking her child to the doctor, they
come to a distinct place which is a dividing line: the city becomes a
massive block of cold stone and plaster, as opposed to the more flexi-
ble brush and dirt houses of the natives. As an example of the city's
buildings, Kino's hut is compared to the doctor's house. The doctor's
house and all of the other houses are isolated by huge stone fences
and an iron gate, and the natives can hear "caged birds" singing
somewhere inside. Thus, the physical structure blocks the natives
from any direct communication with the town people; the town
dwellers seem themselves like caged birds, in contrast to the natives
who live so close to nature.

Steinbeck's social comment is seen in the confrontation between
the two races. Immediately, Kino thinks of the doctor as an enemy.
The doctor is a member of the race who "for nearly four hundred
years had beaten and starved and robbed and despised Kino's race,
and frightened it . . ." so that when Kino reaches the doctor's house,

the "music of the enemy beat in his ears." But in spite of the hatred Kino feels, he still takes off his hat out of forced subservience.

Whereas Kino and his race represent the natural, the descriptions of the doctor suggest that he represents everything that is not natural. All of the natural world has been bred out of him, and he is totally separated from all natural emotions. Therefore, since Kino cannot pay for his child's treatment, the doctor feels no touch of humanity toward the poverty-stricken young family. With his red silk dressing gown and his silver cups and his delicate eggshell china, he is completely opposite to the strong and masculine Kino.

Kino's hand, injured when he smashed it against the gate of the doctor's house, will bother him throughout the novella, and it will serve as a constant reminder of the falseness of the civilized world.

Steinbeck uses the other members of the community in much the way that the Chorus is used in Greek drama. Classical Greek tragedies included a group of actors called the Chorus, whose functions, among others, included informing the audience of the climate of opinion that prevailed among the common people, making philosophic and general comments on the main action of the play as it unfolded and predicting doom or catastrophe for the protagonists. Kino's neighbors serve a similar function throughout the novella.

CHAPTER TWO

In contrast to the first chapter, this chapter takes us out into the Gulf, where the Pearl of the World is to be found. Along the shore, the graceful old canoes are silent, but the Gulf itself is teeming with sea life of various kinds: brown algae floats upward and supports little sea horses while poisonous fish lie "on the bottom in the eel-grass beds," and bright swimming crabs and many other varieties of sea life contend with each other in the battle of survival. Into this alien world come Kino and Juana. This morning, they are far behind the others because of the attention required by Coyotito.

Kino's canoe, which is "at once property and a source of food," has been in his family for two generations. The irony here is, of course, that the canoe represents a continuation of the family tradition, since it belonged first to Kino's father and before that to his grandfather, and yet at the end of the story, Kino will have neither a child nor a canoe to pass on to another generation.

Juana gathers some brown seaweed and makes a "flat damp poultice," which she applies to Coyotito's swollen shoulder. Note that Steinbeck says that this primitive treatment was as good a remedy as any other, or probably better than any remedy that the doctor in town could give. This should be remembered, for in the next chapter the doctor does administer something to Coyotito and it makes him very ill — until the doctor returns and gives him something else to counteract the first dose.

The oyster bed where Kino dives is the same bed which once furnished enough pearls to make the King of Spain rich enough to become a great power in Europe. Steinbeck then explains how a pearl is formed. When a grain of sand begins to irritate the oyster's inner folds of muscle, it emits a layer of secretion which surrounds the grain of sand and this emission, once started, continues until there is a great pearl. Ironically, out of the pain of the oyster, there emerges one of nature's beautiful objects — the pearl.

As Kino begins to dive, he remembers that his people have sung a song for almost every occasion in the world. Now as he dives, he seems to hear the *Song of the Pearl That Might Be*. As he collects oysters, he suddenly spots one that is larger than all the others, lying in a very isolated spot. Through a glimpse of light, he thinks that he spots a large pearl inside. He quickly pulls the oyster away and surfaces to the boat where Juana can sense an air of excitement as Kino climbs into the boat. Kino, however, does not want to open the big oyster yet — one must "be very tactful with God or the gods." After a bit, Juana prompts him to open it, and sure enough, there is the greatest pearl in the world. It is as large as a sea gull's egg, as perfect as the moon and as refined as if it were made of silver incandescence.

After Juana approaches to look at the pearl, she instinctively goes to Coyotito and discovers that the swelling in the baby's shoulder has disappeared. Kino, out of joy over the pearl and because of his joy over Coyotito's recovery, lets out a howl so loud that the rest of the pearl divers race to his boat.

As in the first chapter, this one also begins by describing some aspect of the town. It is a cinematic technique — that is, the author eventually focuses in on the canoe on the beach. The canoes become representative of the continuance of the primitive family, since each family has a canoe that has been a part of the family for generations.

The factual descriptions of the beach include the brown algae and the various flora and fauna. The hazy mirage over the beach provides the author with a starting point for a digression on the imagination, a new way of viewing the Gulf. All these things seem unreal and have the vagueness of a dream, suggesting that these primitive people trust things of the imagination and of the spirit. This is, in some ways, a description of Kino's mind because before he opens the pearl, he has visions and dreams of what he is going to do with the money that he will receive. Kino's primitive imagination allows him to respond to the wonders of the pearl *before* he actually opens the oyster.

Steinbeck sometimes offers a digressive element from the actual story, and usually these are indicative of Steinbeck's attitude toward some aspect of the story. They are often slanted against the church or society or, as in this chapter, they provide a bit of factual information about how the oyster forms a pearl.

Immediately before finding the pearl, there is the introduction of another song, the *Song of the Pearl That Might Be.* All of Kino's hopes are centered on finding the pearl so that his son, Coyotito, can receive proper medical treatment now, and later Coyotito can receive a good education in the style of the conquerors.

When they find the pearl, both Juana and Kino exercise great tact in not angering the gods by showing their eagerness to open the big oyster. The reader is to understand this as primitive superstition. Since the pearl is to be the means whereby Coyotito will receive an education, it is ironic that the superstition is important here. In addition to the concept of superstition, the delay may also be seen merely as a device for arousing suspense.

Note the descriptions of the pearl. It is first described as "the great pearl, perfect as the moon." Now it is a force for great good; it will only gradually become a force for great evil. As Kino holds the pearl in the same hand that he smashed against the doctor's gate, there is the suggestion that the pearl will ultimately be used to prevent such injustices. In the hands of Kino, the simple and primitive man, the pearl is a force for great good, but when the pearl becomes known to the more civilized world, it will then become a force for evil. Both of the first two chapters end with the mention of Kino's wounded hand, a hand which will influence his actions throughout the rest of the novella. The goodness of the pearl is represented by the fact that young Coyotito's wound has disappeared.

CHAPTER THREE

Steinbeck begins this chapter by describing the town in terms of an animal or as some type of biological organism. In the "Introduction" section, it was noted that one interpretation for this novel is an ecological interpretation, one in which we observe that every part of a complex pattern is related to every other part. As noted elsewhere, Steinbeck had previously made a study of the ecological relations of the living organisms in the Gulf of lower California. In his work *The Sea Of Cortez*, Steinbeck writes about the activities of schools of fish as an organized group:

> The schools swam, marshalled and patrolled. They turned and dived as a unit. In their millions they followed a pattern minute as to direction and depth and speed. There must be some fallacy in our thinking of these fish as individuals. Their functions in the school are in some as yet unknown way as controlled as though the school were one unit.

At the beginning of Chapter Three, Steinbeck also writes that the "town is a thing like a colonial animal." Before Kino reaches home, the news of the discovery of the pearl has spread like the "nerves of the town were pulsing and vibrating with the news." Steinbeck is showing the effect of the discovery of the great pearl upon the life of the entire organism—the town. He then offers the response of the various members of the town: the priest remembers certain repairs on the church that are needed; the doctor announces that Coyotito is a patient of his; the beggars remember that a poor man suddenly invested with a fortune is a generous man; the pearl buyers long to get their hands on this great pearl so they can escape from their positions and make a new start.

Steinbeck's sociological views are offered when he writes that the individual pearl buyers are all subservient to one buyer, and that each buyer is another "arm" representing the key pearl buyer. As the news of the great pearl spreads, one man suddenly becomes every man's enemy, and that man is Kino, who owns the pearl. The pearl stirs up "something infinitely black and evil in the town."

Kino is ignorant of the jealousy and hatred that is caused by his discovery of the pearl. His first thoughts are to be married in the church, to buy a new harpoon and a rifle, and then, the greatest of all visions — Kino's son, Coyotito, will be able to go to school and learn how to read and write; thus, Coyotito will be able to help free his people from the walls of ignorance and illiteracy which have kept them imprisoned for so long.

The priest pays Kino and Juana a visit, and he reminds Kino to give thanks for the pearl. But the music of the *Song of Evil* and the music of the *Song of the Enemy* almost drown out the priest's words because he quotes things from the books that Kino cannot know until Coyotito learns to read.

Next, the doctor and his servant arrive. Even though Kino knows that Coyotito is now completely well, the doctor is able to use superstition to frighten Kino into letting him attend the child by suggesting many different evil ways that the poison of the scorpion can work against Coyotito. Kino cannot take a chance. He cannot pit his "certain ignorance against this man's possible knowledge." The doctor obviously tricks Kino by showing him false evidence of the poisoning and he "skillfully" administers some type of drug in the form of a white powder, predicting that within an hour Coyotito will be feeling the results of the scorpion's poison. It is obvious even to Kino that the doctor has given the baby something to make him sick, but again his ignorance is too great to combat the doctor's tricks.

Soon Coyotito becomes flushed, spasms begin, and he becomes very sick. For his wife's sake, Kino says that the doctor was right, but in his heart, Kino is suspicious of the doctor, for he keeps remembering the white powder which the doctor gave his son. After an hour, the doctor returns, gives the baby another kind of medicine, and the spasms subside. The doctor wonders when he will be paid, and it is then that Kino tells him that tomorrow he will sell a beautiful pearl. The doctor is surprised and offers to keep the pearl in a safe place for Kino. When Kino refuses, the doctor taunts him, knowing that Kino will reveal the hiding place of the pearl by a quick secret glance toward the pearl, which is exactly what happens. The doctor leaves, knowing where the pearl is buried.

At bedtime, Kino hides the pearl under his mat on the earthen floor. His dreams of Coyotito's reading great books, however, are suddenly interrupted by the presence of someone else in the hut.

Pulling his knife, Kino strikes out at the figure, and in one blow he feels his knife draw blood, but at the same time he himself is struck a powerful blow on the head. Juana lights their only candle and swabs the blood from Kino's head. Juana then senses the evil of the pearl, and she pleads: "This pearl is like a sin! It will destroy us. . . . Let us throw it back into the sea. . . ." Kino, however, is determined that their son will become educated, and he refuses to listen to Juana's pleas that the pearl will destroy them all—"even our son."

At dawn, Kino digs up the pearl and gazes at its beauty, and he dreams of the promise of the relief that it will bring them. For that reason, after a horrible night, the new day promises only hope.

As noted elsewhere, the symbolic value of the pearl is beginning to take on various meanings, as a symbolic pearl has throughout all of Western literature. In biblical literature, a pearl of great price is something that is bought at great sacrifice, and it brings the kingdom of heaven. Kino also thinks of the pearl as bringing all types of rewards to him, but instead, it will function only to destroy everything that he previously held valuable. The concept of the pearl as something of great value is often found in medieval literature, and in American literature, Nathaniel Hawthorne uses the name Pearl to suggest that Hester Prynne bought her daughter at the great price of her own reputation.

Throughout this chapter, we are made aware of the chorus of villagers who function to express the various reactions to the great pearl. We see first Kino's reactions to the pearl, and then we see how the villagers react to it. The difference between the two reactions is that there exists a vast gulf between Kino's simple optimistic expectations and the prophecies of doom as expressed by the villagers.

In addition to the general reactions evoked by the discovery of the pearl, Steinbeck gives the various individual reactions. First, the priest wonders if Kino will contribute to the church. The doctor thinks of his past life in Paris and what he could do now with the money. The beggars remember that a man made newly rich is often generous and that they may receive alms from Kino. Each of the pearl buyers thinks of the pearl and wishes that he could get it in order to make a new start in life. In general, the pearl affects the entire town and becomes *everyone's* pearl or everyone's dream of greatness.

As the pearl thus becomes the "property" of everyone, everyone begins to turn against Kino. He becomes "every man's enemy," and the evil caused by the reports of the pearl is like the scorpion which bit little Coyotito.

After giving the town's reaction, Steinbeck then turns his attention to Kino and his plans for the pearl. Kino constantly thinks of the good that the pearl will bring him. Note that he thinks first of a church ceremony, then of an education for his son. He sees that an education will set them free. This idea reappears later in the chapter when the doctor arrives and tells Kino that the baby is sick. Kino realizes the importance of knowing what is "in the books," but he doesn't know whether or not to trust the doctor; he is finally forced to do so, however, so that his son can get an education and can determine whether the books are true.

Notice that throughout the chapter, there are many references to Kino's wounded hand. This was the hand that was injured, in anger, when the doctor refused to see Kino; now he holds the pearl in this hand. The pearl in the wounded hand suggests the contrasting effects brought about by Kino's discovery.

The musical motifs also play an important part in this chapter. Often a musical motif is used to give Kino's true feelings. For example, when the priest arrives, "the melody of the morning, the music of evil, of the enemy sounded." This motif suggests that Kino is aware of the hypocrisy of the priest and knows that the priest is also an enemy. The same musical motif sounds when the doctor arrives later in the chapter.

As the news of the pearl spreads, Kino feels more and more isolated from the community. He takes refuge in the family, and the *Song of the Family* becomes a strong motif. This motif is interrupted by the arrival of the doctor, and then Kino is filled with hatred and fear. The doctor talks about poison, and Steinbeck indicates that the only poison now is that which is brought by the doctor. It is intimated that Coyotito is well until the doctor gives him medication that actually makes him sick again. Thus, the evil is brought by the vile white powder given to Coyotito.

Steinbeck uses some basic analogies to suggest the destructive force of the doctor. He offers a digression about how schools of small fish try to escape from larger fish, but are nevertheless slaughtered by the larger fish.

At the end of the chapter, the first statement appears that the pearl is evil rather than good. Until now, Kino was thinking only of the good that it could bring, but more evil is happening to him than good. Juana then declares, "This pearl is like a sin! It will destroy us." But in contrast to Juana's thought, the chapter ends by emphasizing the beauty of the pearl and the possible good which it can do. At this fulcrum point, the novella could go toward good effects or toward evil effects.

CHAPTER FOUR

It was noted that the town was very much like a type of organism in the last chapter. Here again, Steinbeck begins this chapter by comparing the town to a larger unit, or organism, in which no single action is separate from any other. Only when one person deviates from the general pattern of the rest of the unit is there a significant change. In this chapter, Kino will step out of the known and trusted pattern of behavior; he will no longer be a part of the larger organism; as such, he will be more vulnerable to the enemy since he does not have the collective protection of the entire organism. Significantly, the entire town knows that Kino is going to sell his pearl today.

This "organism" image is carried through and expanded to include the pearl buyers. There were once many pearl buyers bidding against one another, but now there "was only one pearl buyer with many hands," and the pearl buyers sitting and waiting for Kino already knew what each would offer for the Pearl of the World.

On the morning that Kino is to sell the pearl, the other divers do not go out to dive; this is to be a special day in the life of the town. Kino and Juana dress themselves and Coyotito in their best clothes and begin the trip to the pearl buyers, followed by all of the rest of the village. Here, we have the second of several processional scenes. Yesterday, they walked in the same procession to see the doctor, and they were defeated and turned away. Today, they go in a triumphant mood, fully aware of the treasure they have that will bring them wealth and respect.

In the processional, Juan Tomas walks beside Kino and reminds Kino of the old story of how years ago the "old ones" thought of a way to outwit the pearl buyers by sending one of their own to the large town to sell their collected pearls. The first man failed to return; they sent another with their collected pearls and he too failed to return.

They then abandoned the idea and returned to selling their pearls to the pearl buyers. Kino, of course, has heard the story already; the priest, the Father, tells it every year. According to the priest, the failure was "a punishment on those who tried to leave their station." The priest made it clear that God intends the peons to remain in their stations in life, and if someone tries to rise above their station, it is an invitation for disaster. This view of the priest, of course, shows him to be simply a tool of the wealthy pearl buyers; he is not concerned at all with the social welfare of his parishioners.

The news of Kino's impending arrival in town has already reached the pearl buyers, along with reports on the loveliness of the pearl. One of the pearl buyers, a fatherly, jovial man, sits in his office playing a disappearing trick with coins while he waits for Kino. The mere fact that this pearl buyer is playing a game in which a coin disappears, a game used at cheap carnivals to cheat innocent bystanders, sets the tone for the entire pearl-buying operation.

When Kino arrives with the pearl, his neighbors wait just within hearing distance, outside the office. The pearl buyer looks casually at the pearl and shows no expression on his face, yet his hands, hidden behind him, are trembling. Then the buyer offers a very small sum, a thousand pesos, for the Pearl of the World. He maintains that the pearl is too big – the pearl is a curiosity that no one will buy. Kino knows that he is being cheated; meanwhile, the pearl buyer sends for the other buyers to confirm his offer. While they are waiting for the other buyers, the neighbors discuss the offer. They are puzzled; in contrast, the pearl buyer cannot keep his eyes off the pearl.

When the other three pearl buyers arrive, they carry through with their pre-arranged, assigned roles. One will make no offer at all; the pearl is a monstrosity. The second buyer maintains that the pearl will "die" in a few months. The third buyer offers five hundred pesos. The pearl buyers, however, have misjudged their client: Kino announces that he will go to the capital and sell the pearl. Quickly, the main pearl buyer raises his offer to fifteen hundred pesos, but it is too late; Kino leaves.

Back in their brush houses, the neighbors discuss the events. They are divided in their opinions: some feel that Kino is being cheated; some feel that he is going against the system, and some think that he is foolish because fifteen hundred pesos is more money than he has ever had. Kino, however, feels alienated from everything: according to Steinbeck, Kino "has lost one world and had not gained another."

That night after Kino and Juana are in bed, Kino hears some noises outside. He takes his knife and goes to investigate. Inside, Juana hears the noises of a violent struggle, and she takes a stone and goes to Kino's aid, but it is too late. Kino is lying on the ground, bloody, with most of his clothes half-torn off him. His assailants have escaped, and Kino cannot identify them. Again, Juana pleads with Kino to destroy the pearl – it is wicked. But Kino still sees the pearl as the only means of insuring Coyotito's education, and so he resolves to go to the capital to sell the pearl.

As a parallel to the last chapter, Kino has had the pearl with him for two nights, and he has been severely beaten on both nights. In both cases, the assailants are some unknown forces of evil from the darkness. It would be too simplistic to say that the assailants in Chapter Three came from the doctor, and that these came from the pearl buyers. Steinbeck wants us to see these as simply forces which are destined to try and destroy Kino. In the same way, the trackers who follow Kino in the next chapter will never be identified; they will remain merely abstract forces of destruction and evil.

This chapter is one of Steinbeck's most direct criticisms of the unjustice of the social system of Kino's village. As noted previously, the priest joins with the existing powers to emphasize the manner in which the Indians must yield to the authority of the pearl buyers because, according to him, it is "God's will" that they must stay in their divinely appointed station in life. Kino, according to this theory, is defying God and the system by trying to rise above his "assigned" place in life. Likewise, the pearl buyers have organized to get the pearls from the Indian divers at the lowest price. The Indian men know this, but they can do nothing about it: in "four hundred years Kino's people had learned only one defense – a slight slitting of the eyes and a slight tightening of the lips and a retirement. Nothing could break down this wall. . . ."

The town as an organism or unit is presented again when the entire town deserts its usual occupation; the beach, which is usually teeming with activity, is isolated. Now, there is a procession straggling into the town. As noted above, the first procession occurred when Juana and Kino went as suppliants to the doctor in town, accompanied by their sympathetic neighbors; this action ended with Kino's frustration and a bleeding fist. This procession now is of a different spirit. Today, Kino has something which the town wants, and the people who accompany Kino are no longer so friendly. Thus, we should be prepared for another procession, a third procession, when Kino will return from the mountains as a defeated man.

After Kino refuses to sell the pearl, his brother tells him: "You have defied not the pearl buyers, but the whole structure, the whole way of life, and I am afraid for you." This idea should be correlated with the sermon preached every year by the priest when he advises each man to "remain faithful to his post and . . . not go running about, else the castle is in danger from the assaults of Hell." The priest is not truly concerned with the social situation; rather, he is attempting to keep the natives in line. Kino's brother, Juan, fears for Kino because Kino believes that he is a man with the right to revolt against dishonesty to prove his dignity as a man.

CHAPTER FIVE

This brief chapter piles one evil thing on top of another evil thing, and finally Kino is reduced to desperation. Significantly, everything evil that happens to him is directly related to the Pearl of the World, and Juana knows this. At the beginning of the chapter, she silently rises from her sleep, goes quietly to the fireplace stone and removes the great pearl. Then, like a shadow, she disappears through the doorway. A rage surges in Kino, and he catches up with her at the beach just at the moment that her hand is raised to throw the pearl back into the Gulf. Kino strikes her; "his teeth [are] bared. He [hisses] at her like a snake." Already, there is a major change occurring within Kino; he is becoming more and more like an animal — even in his treatment of Juana who, because of her upbringing, accepts such treatment. She knows that there is murder in the heart of her husband, and she accepts it without understanding it. In the same way, she knows that she needs a man; she does not know *why*, but she knows that Kino is a man, and she cannot live without a man.

For the third time, Kino is attacked by some dark, unknown figures. This time the pearl is knocked from his hand, but this time, Kino is able to shove his knife into one of the assailants before the others knock him unconscious. He remembers hands and fingers, however, searching his body before he loses total consciousness.

When Juana recovers from the blows that Kino gave her, she follows her husband and finds him lying unconscious on the path, with a dead stranger close beside him. Juana now realizes that something of the old peace, the peace that existed before the time of the pearl, is gone forever. It is ironic that only a day before, they thought that all future times would be counted in terms of all the happiness they would have as a result of Kino's finding the pearl. "They knew that time would now date from Kino's pearl, and that they would discuss this moment for many years to come." In contrast, the future is now to be counted in terms of sadness and misfortune from the day of the discovery of the pearl.

Even though Juana had earlier tried to throw the pearl back into the Gulf, now when Kino recovers and thinks that he has lost the pearl, Juana, who found it behind a rock, returns it to him, telling him that they must leave their village and go away because of the dead stranger. Kino sends Juana after their meager supplies while he goes to make the boat ready for the journey, but he discovers that someone has smashed a large hole in the bottom of the boat. Kino's reactions are important here; they represent the primitive values of his culture. He feels that the killing of a family boat ("the canoe of his grandfather") is a greater crime than the killing of a person because a person has a family that can revenge him. Following through with this logic, Kino knows that he himself could never, even for a moment, think of taking someone else's boat for his escape, even though there are other boats for the taking.

Suddenly, as Kino and Juana return to their hut, they see that their brush house is in flames. This is their third encounter with evil forces within a short time. When Kino asks Juana who did it, she cannot identify anyone—it is "the dark ones" is all she can answer. Quickly, before any of the neighbors can see them, Kino and Juana take the baby and go to Kino's brother's brush house; there, they hide all day long. During the day, Kino's brother, Juan Tomás, lets the other villagers think that Kino has escaped and gone, and he also borrows certain basic provisions for Kino's escape, even though he also feels that the pearl is now an evil thing. Kino, however, maintains that the pearl has become a part of his soul. Were he to give it up now, it would be as though he were giving up a part of his soul.

In terms of the total structure of the novel, Chapter Four ended with Kino's decision to go away and with Juana's expressing again her fear of the pearl. Chapter Five now opens with Juana's attempt to remove the tension caused by the pearl by throwing it into the sea. Here is the first indication that the family is breaking apart.

As noted above, when Kino attacks Juana, he is responding as though he were a savage, and the imagery which Steinbeck uses is that of an animal protecting himself. Kino feels that his manhood is involved with the pearl. If he gives it up, he will be admitting defeat and thus will lose his position as "the man" – note also that he emphasizes several times, "I am a man." Furthermore, if he allows Juana to decide about the pearl – that is, if he is left out of the final disposition of the pearl, he will no longer be the head of the house. Finally, the pearl has meant so much to Kino in his dreams that he cannot afford to sacrifice those dreams easily. He will pit himself against the mountains and against all forces in order to keep the pearl.

We should be aware that Juana passively accepts her beating. Her response is "sheeplike" because she knows that she has gone beyond the limited scope of the primitive wife. Because the characters are uncommunicative – all but mute – the author must find other means than speech to let the reader know their thoughts. As noted previously, the musical motifs frequently reveal Kino's emotional state when he has no words to express it. Thus, the manner in which Juana recovers from Kino's attack shows that she has accepted her position and will face what troubles the pearl will now bring to them. These troubles arrive almost immediately as Juana sees a stranger "with dark shiny fluid" on his body lying in the darkness. The description in this passage is highly effective because it stimulates our imaginations and emotions. It aligns the reader with Kino's determination to fight and, at the same time, makes us highly sympathetic to Juana's desire to be rid of the pearl.

Immediately after the attack, Juana realizes that the safety of the "old life was gone forever." She then "abandon[s] the past instantly" and sees that she must now rely upon new and strange forces that nothing in their past life has prepared them to encounter.

Kino, discovering that his canoe has been destroyed, feels that the "killing of a man was not so evil as the killing of a boat." We have seen earlier that the boat is a symbol of the family, its heritage and its power to continue. This reverence for the canoe tells us a great deal about Kino's society and about his cultural environment. The canoe is the only item of great value to him because it represents the importance of his culture, and it is something which he could pass on to Coyotito with great pride. Its destruction suggests the forces that are aligning themselves against Kino and which will ultimately drive him or pursue him into the mountain.

Next, the unknown "dark ones" set the house on fire. This vague and forbidding description adds a symbolic dimension. The "dark ones" are evil itself – the forces of darkness. By now, Kino's boat and his house have been destroyed, and he is left alone to face the dark forces.

Kino's determination to keep the pearl is the beginning of his destruction. He sees the pearl as a gift; he feels that he should hold on to it or else he will endanger his relationship with the gods. Similarly, the final exchange between Kino and Juan Tomás indicates that the pearl is more than a mere physical pearl or a treasure. Kino identifies it with his soul. "If I give it up I shall lose my soul." The truth is the opposite – in keeping the pearl, he is losing his soul, and only in the act of throwing it away will he be able to save his soul.

CHAPTER SIX

Chapter Six begins with Kino and his family making an exodus from his known world to enter a new, strange world where they do not know their way. They are leaving the safety and the assurance of one life because of Kino's fierce desire to start a new life. The pearl, if it can be sold, will allow Coyotito to go to school and to be a part of this new world, but first Kino must make his way through a strange and alien world.

As they begin their journey, "some ancient thing stirred in Kino. . . ." They avoid the center of town because they are afraid that they might be noticed – ironically, only two days ago they led a long procession down to the center of the town when they sought the doctor's help. Now they are sneaking out of the town and heading toward Loreto, where "the miraculous Virgin has her station." This irony becomes apparent later when *nothing* will be helpful to Kino and Juana.

At first, Kino is happy for the wind; it will cover up their tracks, but in a short time the wind dies down, and he knows there will be footprints left behind them. Still, as he is escaping, the "music of the pearl was triumphant in Kino's head." Each time they change their direction, Kino returns with a brush and sweeps their footsteps away.

Since they are far from the Gulf now, the sun is hot, and Kino lectures Juana on the kinds of poisonous plants to be avoided. Juana wonders if they will be followed; Kino knows that they will be followed because the pearl must be extremely valuable or else so many people would not have tried such desperate measures to take the pearl away from him.

Since they travel during the night, at dawn they conceal themselves in a clearing and settle down for the day; Juana and Coyotito sleep, and Kino watches over them. When Juana awakens, she wonders if it was the pearl dealers who attacked Kino, but he was not able to see or identify his attackers. In the past and here in this chapter, Kino's enemies will remain simply the "dark ones," forces or men who are never identified.

Kino sleeps and dreams of the great pearl, of being married in the church and of giving Coyotito an education. He awakens suddenly from a restless sleep and is immediately alerted to some noise. Instructing Juana to keep Coyotito quiet, he cautiously creeps to the clearing, "an animal light" in his eyes. Steinbeck is now beginning to emphasize that Kino is becoming more and more like a hunted animal; and increasingly, Kino's actions will be seen in terms of a desperate, trapped animal. Suddenly, he sees the trackers who are following him—two men on foot, following his tracks and one man on horseback carrying a rifle, which shines in the reflection of the sun. Kino knows how good these trackers are: "They were as sensitive as hounds"; furthermore, they can read almost invisible signs and determine the direction of the pursued. Kino knows that escape from these expert trackers is probably impossible. Thus, he must make plans to protect his family against them. As the trackers come near enough for Kino to see their legs, he watches them return to the place where he brushed out their tracks earlier. Then they move on, but Kino knows that they will circle and come back to the same place and eventually pick up his and Juana's tracks. He panics and tells Juana to pack, and that he will let them take him prisoner. Juana reminds him that the trackers will not let either her or Coyotito live.

Then, not even bothering to conceal their direction, they head for the higher mountains. Steinbeck describes their flight this way: "And Kino ran for the high place, as nearly all animals do when they are pursued." Again, he continues to emphasize the animal aspect of Kino's behavior.

When they reach the first rise, Kino tries to persuade Juana to hide in a crevice with Coyotito and let him lead the trackers away, up into the mountains; then he will return. Juana is too frightened and refuses to be left alone. Three times she refuses before Kino relinquishes. They then move into the mountains, where Kino knows that they will find water. When they reach the small spring, they refresh themselves with cool water, and Kino peers out behind him. He can see the trackers far away. Even though the trackers are "little more than little dots" on the landscape, Kino knows that they will be where he now is by evening. He and Juana decide to hide in little erosion caves. He places Juana and Coyotito in one of these small caves, then he returns to the spring and makes all sorts of false trails up the other side of the mountain. He tells Juana that when the trackers follow the false trails, they can then slip away down to the lowlands again." Kino, however, is frightened that Coyotito may cry, and so he relegates to Juana the responsibility of seeing that Coyotito makes no noise.

When the trackers arrive, they immediately see the false tracks up the other side of the mountain. The trackers, however, decide to camp for the night beside the spring until morning. This is bad; Kino knows that he and his family cannot stay concealed and quiet throughout the night. He decides, therefore, that he must attack the trackers, killing, first, the one with the rifle, then the other two. If he is killed, Juana is to remain hidden and then escape when the trackers leave: "There is no choice . . . it is the only way, "Kino says, "They will find us in the morning." Tenderly and fumblingly, he touches Coyotito and then Juana's cheek; then he removes his torn and ragged white clothes so that his brown skin will be difficult to see in the darkness. As he leaves, Juana moves to the entrance of the cave to watch him. (Ironically, had Juana remained in the back of the cave, instead of moving forward to watch Kino, Coyotito's life would have been saved by the protection of the cave.)

Kino moves slowly and deliberately down the mountain toward the camp fire, placing each foot down with extreme care so as not to turn over even the smallest stone. His knife is hanging down his back so that it will not hit a stone and make a noise. As he inches within a short distance from the tracker with the rifle (the others are sleeping), the moon begins to rise, and Kino is desperate. He cannot wait until the full moon; he must attack now. Suddenly from above, there comes a "little murmuring cry." The watcher thinks it sounds like a cry, almost like a human—like a baby." One of the others, who is now awake, says that sometimes a "coyote pup cries like a baby." (Ironically, the noise does come from Coyotito, whose name means "little coyote.") As the watcher raises his gun to fire in that direction, Kino, like a wild animal, strikes at the man with the rifle: "Kino was in mid-leap when the gun crashed and [his] great knife swung and crunched hollowly. It bit through neck and deep into chest." He grabs the rifle and immediately kills the second man. As the third man is frantically scrambling up the mountain to escape, Kino deliberately ("Kino had become as cold and deadly as steel") aims and fires at the enemy, who tumbles back down the mountain. Only then is Kino aware of a sound—some wrong signal—it is "the keening, moaning, rising hysterical cry from the little cave in the side of the stone mountain, the cry of death."

With the passing of time, everyone remembers how Kino and Juana returned to the town of La Paz; their return has become a part of the folklore and legend of the town. Steinbeck tells us that it was late in the afternoon when they arrived back in town. They were walking side by side, rather than in single file, as is customary. Their suffering has removed traditional barriers and has made them equal.

Kino carries a long rifle across his arm, and Juana carries a "small limp heavy bundle," a bundle which holds Coyotito's dead body. Her face is "hard and lined and leathery with fatigue . . . and she [is] remote and removed." They both seem to be removed from all human experiences. They walk through the town and through the village like well-made wooden dolls, neither glancing in either direction nor greeting any of the villagers.

When they come to the beach, Kino removes the pearl and stares at its surface; there, he sees all of the evil that has happened to him—"in the surface of the pearl he [sees] Coyotito lying in the little cave with the top of his head shot way." He gives the pearl to Juana to throw away, but she refuses saying "No, you." Kino draws back his arm and hurls the pearl as far out into the Gulf as he can. It sinks into the water and settles down to the sandy bottom among the waving branches of the water plants. "And the music of the pearl drifted to a whisper and disappeared."

In this final chapter of the novel, Steinbeck begins his narrative by having his characters make an exodus from the town, and he ends the chapter (and the novel) with the return of the travelers to the town, thus making the chapter circular in structure. Furthermore the entire chapter is circular in motion since the central part of the chapter emphasizes the various circular motions that Kino undertakes to elude the trackers.

At the beginning of the chapter, Kino is very determined that he will save his Pearl of the World. As Steinbeck indicates, there is something primitive in Kino as he is determined, at first, to protect his pearl at all costs. Steinbeck also seems to be implying that as society turns against Kino and tries to rob him of his pearl, then Kino must become more like an animal. For a point in contrast, the reader should read and compare this novella with Steinbeck's classic short story "Flight," a story which tells the parable of a simple young peasant (Pepé), who is almost identical to Kino. In this short story, the young native is forced to kill a man who threatens his life; he is then pursued by a posse, and he, like Kino, becomes gradually more and more like a hunted animal; and whereas in *The Pearl*, the pursuers are never identified, remaining always a dark, remote force of evil, likewise, in the story "Flight," the posse is never seen or identified — it always remains a distant, threatening force which ultimately kills the young man.

The change in Kino from a man into an animal is indicated by the changing meanings of the pearl and other things important to Kino. For example, when Kino looks into the pearl to find the visions he first saw in it, the evil which the pearl has brought has distorted the visions so that a bad image is substituted for each of the original good images. The gleaming rifle becomes a murdered man; the wedding in the church becomes Juana's beaten face. Coyotito's education becomes the baby's sick and fevered face. The music of the pearl becomes the music of evil. Notice that these ideas are expressed in a one-to-one relationship.

As the trackers track down Kino and Juana, Kino becomes more like a wild animal. He and his family are no longer a part of a safe community; instead, they become objects of a primitive hunt.

The ground which they cross is barren and dry while their destination, the mountain, is cool and welcoming. There is clearly a symbolic identification with death (sterility, desert heat, and dehydration) and life (fertility, life-giving moisture, and coolness). Thus, there is an ironic reversal in that they find death, not life, in the mountains. This supports the irony that the great pearl brings evil and disaster, not happiness.

More specifically, the spring is described in terms of a place of rest and of life. But it is also a place of death. It is where animals come for water, but it is also a place where certain animals kill other animals. For Kino, it will be a temporary refuge, but later it will be the site of his own son's death.

Kino and Juana return to the town carrying a bundle. It is not until later that it is realized that the bundle contains the dead baby, Coyotito. We realize the Kino won his fight against the three trackers but in doing so, he lost his son and, with him, all of his dreams. The pearl was to have secured for Coyotito a good education and for Kino, a good rifle. Kino does enter the town carrying a rifle but this, in terms of the death of his son, is completely meaningless.

With their entrance into the town, a third procession occurs. This time, Juana is walking side by side with Kino. Both have learned much from the tragedy that they have shared. They have "gone through pain and [have] come out on the other side." There is almost a magical protection about them.

Kino and Juana go straight to the Gulf, where Kino gives her the pearl to throw away. This time, Juana returns it to Kino knowing that he alone must decide what to do with the pearl. He draws back his arm and flings the pearl with all his might. Finally, it settles to the bottom of the ocean.

CHARACTERS AND CHARACTERIZATION

As noted in the "Life and Background" section at the beginning of these Notes, Steinbeck was always completely familiar with his subject matter, and as was pointed out, before he wrote *The Grapes of Wrath*, he went first to Oklahoma and lived and traveled with a family of "Okies" until he had experienced all of the scenes that he included in his novel. Likewise, the characters in *The Pearl* are also based on first-hand, authentic experience. This is not to say that Steinbeck lived with the Indians in and around La Paz, but the entire story is based on Steinbeck's actual observations.

It was during Steinbeck's trip with Ed Ricketts that he met these types of people and heard the legend of the great pearl. In *The Sea of Cortez*, which recounts in detail the adventures and experiments along the Gulf of Mexico, Steinbeck describes the local Indians whom he met; they were totally illiterate, extremely poor, and lacking in any knowledge of the larger world, but nevertheless they possessed a sense of honesty, dignity, and humanity. They were, as Steinbeck points out, subjected to all sorts of primitive religious beliefs mixed with Christian teachings; they were superstitious, as are many uneducated natives, but beyond these limitations, these people inspired Steinbeck by their basic adherence to traditions, to courtesy, to integrity, and to humanity. They were constantly cheated by forces in society such as the pearl buyers, and constantly humiliated by forces, represented in *The Pearl* by the priest, "the Father," (he tells them to keep in their social places and not to question those in power—such as the pearl buyers) and by the doctor. This injustice aroused within Steinbeck a sense of indignation at the injustices that these simple people had to endure. Thus, most of the characters in the novel are depicted not as full, three-dimensional characters, but as figures possessing certain traits that are representative of a large number of people. Like characters in a parable, they become symbolic of the function which they play in the novel. For example, the pearl buyers are not distinguishable from each other; they represent, instead, a certain force in society which oppresses the Indian divers, and yet they are also victimized by forces above them. Steinbeck conveys the idea that these pearl buyers, if replaced by others, are no different from any other pearl buyers.

KINO

One of the great appeals of *The Pearl* lies in the beautiful and simplistic way that Kino is characterized. However sophisticated one might become, there is always something that one finds appealing in the "noble savage" or the "pristine innocence" of people like Kino, whose life is lived close to the simple harmony of the natural world and who is not affected by the hypocrisies and artificialities of the "civilized world." For example, Kino's simple breakfast of corncake and pulque contrasts well with the opulent decadence of the doctor's breakfast of cocoa served to him in bed in a dainty china cup.

Kino's profession – a simple pearl diver – requires him to be constantly close to nature, and he is constantly affected by natural events; for example, when the sea is rough or the climate is unsuitable, Kino cannot practice his trade. Even though he is on the lowest economic rung of society, he still has a deep sense of human dignity. In fact, he is not even fully aware of how much the townspeople despise and exploit all of his people. Only when the outside forces – whether it be the scorpion, the doctor, or the pearl buyers – intrude upon his life does he then become estranged within his natural surrounding. Otherwise, Kino lives a perfectly harmonious life, both socially and environmentally.

The harmony of his life is also evident in his relationship with his wife, in his devotion to his son, in his kinship with his brother, and in his respect for the traditions of the village. Toward Juana, his wife, he is protective and concerned. He would sacrifice his life for her; yet when she crosses him by trying to throw away the pearl, he can be quite severe with her. When they are trying to escape the trackers (in Chapter Six), Kino is constantly concerned about Juana and Coyotito's safety. At one point, he is even willing to allow himself to be captured so as to protect Juana and Coyotito.

Part of Kino's tragedy is that his entire life is built mainly around his love for his son. Earlier, when the scorpion bit his son, Kino felt completely helpless because he had no money and no credibility with the doctor. His frustration was expressed in smashing his fist against the doctor's door. Then, with the discovery of the pearl, Kino immediately thinks of all the advantages which it will provide for his son. For himself, Kino desires no real personal gain (the rifle he dreams of will only enable him to become a better provider for the family). From the total frustration caused by the scorpion's bite to the elation caused by the discovery of the pearl, Kino's thoughts are always directed toward his son's welfare.

In his kinship with his brother and in his respect for the traditions of the village, Kino is seen in a simple but harmonious relationship. There is no strife between him and his brother. To the contrary, when Kino's brush house is burned, his brother, Juan Tomas, hides the entire family all day long and spends his own day going from one neighbor to another to borrow something, which he then gives to Kino. Likewise, Kino has great respect for the traditions of the village. Even though his own canoe has been destroyed and even though there are other canoes on the beach for the taking, he would never consider taking someone else's canoe; to him, a canoe is a part of one's family heritage and, as such, it is sacred. The destruction of his own canoe, then, had to be perpetrated by someone who was not a member of the village.

Kino's basic response to life and his basic emotions are not always expressed directly. For centuries, Kino's ancestors have composed or created songs to express every possible emotion and to fit every possible occasion. Consequently, from the opening to the closing pages, the songs which Kino hears express his own basic emotions. At the beginning of the novel, as he watches Coyotito playing and Juana going about her morning chores, Kino hears the *Song of the Family*; the mere fact that he hears this song represents the love and contentment that he feels but cannot (or does not) express verbally. Likewise, throughout the section, Kino can express his own fears only by physical actions (smashing his fist on the doctor's door) or by the songs which he hears—the *Song of the Enemy*, and the *Song of Evil*, and others.

At the end of the novel, the readers have a sense that through Kino they have experienced all of the emotions common to mankind—the contentment of the family, the joy and elation of discovering a great treasure, the fears when the family's lives are threatened, the anxiety of being hunted, and the tragedy of losing a loved one. As Kino passes through these emotions, he emerges to represent for us a type of universal person—one who has passed from innocence through evil, and yet has survived to reaffirm his manhood by voluntarily throwing the pearl back into the Gulf.

JUANA

Juana's main function is that of Kino's wife. As a member of a primitive race, the woman is the helpmate of the man. She prepares Kino's breakfast for him while he sits outside the brush house, and she attends to Coyotito's needs at the same time. She seems, at first, to be completely subservient to her husband and without any life of her own. She seems to be only the hardworking and loyal wife to a simple fisherman, and she does not complain about her lowly state. Yet, when the scorpion bites Coyotito, there suddenly emerges a new and different Juana. Even though she prays both to some primitive gods and also to the Virgin Mary before Coyotito is bitten, as soon as the scorpion bites him, she springs to the baby's aid, grabbing him up and sucking the poison from his wound. She is much more effective and practical than is Kino, who expends his fury by grinding the scorpion to a pulp. Juana is much more efficient as she takes control, and to the astonishment of the entire village, she announces that she wants a doctor for the baby – a thing unheard of because the doctor has never visited the peasant village. When she is told that the doctor will not come, without hesitation, she decides that they must take Coyotito to the doctor – an event so strange that the entire village follows along behind them.

On the basis of the above actions, we can see that Juana is not merely the obeying, subservient wife. Instead, there is a determination and an assertiveness which is not usual in women of this type. Her fierce and passionate love for her son is immediately apparent in her actions. Later her hatred for the pearl is apparent because she knows that the pearl threatens her family and, thus, it threatens her entire existence. Obedient as she ususally is, when her world is threatened, she can become as determined and as fierce as a lioness.

Juana, like the other natives, is a product of two civilizations. She is filled with superstitious belief, as is noted when the scorpion bites Coyotito, and when she prays, she invokes the help of her native gods, and, for good measure, she also utters one *Hail Mary*. When Juana discovers that Kino has found the Pearl of the World, she pretends that she does not see this wonderful object because she fears that if she looks and shows too much pleasure, it might displease the gods in power. She believes that it is not "good to want a thing too much. It sometimes drives the luck away." Likewise, she is instinctively afraid of many things – the evil figures lurking in the dark, the evil powers of the pearl, and many other unknown fears. Yet, when her husband is attacked, she picks up a stone and attacks the "evil ones" with all of her fury.

Not all of her actions, however, are based on superstitions. When Coyotito is wounded, she knows that the poultice made from seaweed will be beneficial to him. Here, she uses old and ancient knowledge in order to help her son.

While Juana will revolt from the authority of her husband, as seen when she attempts to throw the pearl back into the Gulf, yet when Kino asserts his power and strikes her, she does not complain – in fact, she accepts his beating of her as proper and in the right order of things. But when he wants to leave her during their escape, she will not allow it even though Kino maintains that it is for her and Coyotito's safety. She is wise enough to know that if the trackers find Kino, they would also find her, and she and Coyotito will be killed.

After the death of Coyotito, Juana walks beside her husband for the first time; their suffering has apparently made them more equal. Yet, when Kino gives the pearl to his wife to throw back into the Gulf, she refuses; symbolically, this act restores to her husband his sense of manhood by allowing him the right to destroy that for which he fought and suffered.

In conclusion, Juana is the prototype of the primitive native wife – strong, loyal, obedient, yet independent and courageous when the occasion demands such qualities. She possesses all of the values which allow this type of person to endure in spite of all obstacles.

THE DOCTOR AND THE PRIEST

Both of these characters are so unsympathetically portrayed that they function only on a symbolic level. The doctor is the representative of another way of life – a way of life connected with the pearl buyers and with foreign elements. He has no redeeming qualities, and his actions show him to be the most despicable, heartless individual that one could encounter.

The mere mention of his name among the villagers creates an aura of fear and awe. He has never made an appearance in the village. Thus, later when he does come to see Coyotito, it is with utmost suspicion that Kino allows him to see his son.

When we first meet the doctor, it is in a rather decadent setting. He is lounging in a silk robe and is being served chocolate on a silver service amidst lush flowers. He is dreaming of a woman with whom he once lived in Paris. Everything about him suggests a person who over-indulges himself and cares nothing about the welfare of anyone else. For example, the contrast between Kino's simple breakfast and the opulence of the doctor's breakfast is one more parallel to contrast the two human beings.

While it is not explicitly stated, the doctor, when he attends Coyotito, obviously gives the baby something that will make him sick enough so that the doctor can return in one hour and pretend to cure the baby of the scorpion bite. Steinbeck has already let us know that the seaweed poultice that Juana applied has taken care of the bite; therefore, the doctor's actions are only acts of inhumanity – acts that totally contradict the ethics of his profession. He then tries slyly to get Kino to give him the pearl for safekeeping; only then is the full extent of the doctor's greed and evil apparent. Using his authorial voice, Steinbeck has the beggars speak of the doctor's character. They knew of "his ignorance, his cruelty, his avarice, his appetites, his sins, his clumsy abortions and the little brown pennies he gave sparingly for alms. They had seen his corpses go into the church." The doctor, then, represents in this novel all of the evil forces working against Kino.

The priest, while not presented as being as evil as the doctor, is shown to be a person not really concerned about the spiritual well-being of his parishioners. He is more a representative of the rich than he is a representative of the church. He has a sermon that he preaches yearly, and the central message of the sermon, with examples, is that all people who are trying to improve themselves are sinning against God because they refuse to accept the station in life that God has assigned to them. When the priest first hears of the great pearl, he does not even know who Kino is; he wonders if he married Kino and Juana, and then he immediately thinks of all the repairs which the church needs and which it can have if he can get Kino's pearl. His visits to the village are so rare that everyone in the village knows *why* he comes to visit Kino.

Given the qualities of the priest, it ultimately becomes ironic that Kino wants to sell the pearl so that he can use the money to be married to Juana in the church and so that Coyotito can be baptized here.

THE SOURCE FOR STEINBECK'S *THE PEARL* AND THE "LEGEND OF THE PEARL OF THE WORLD"

In his prose work *The Sea of Cortez*, a work which describes Steinbeck's and Ed Rickett's explorations in the Gulf of California,

Steinbeck reports a story that he heard in the lower California Peninsula; it was reported as a true story occurring in "La Paz in recent years." Steinbeck writes:

> An Indian boy, by accident, found a pearl of great size, an unbelievable pearl. He knew its value was so great that he need never work again. In this one pearl he had the ability to be drunk as long as he wished, to marry any one of a number of girls, and to make many more a little happy too. In his great pearl lay salvation, for he could in advance purchase masses sufficient to pop him out of purgatory like a squeezed watermelon seed. In addition, he could shift a number of dead relatives a little nearer to Paradise.

The original story continues by pointing out how every pearl buyer to whom he tried to sell the pearl offered such a small price that the young Indian finally refused to sell the pearl and, instead, hid it under a rock. For two nights in a row, the young man was attacked and beaten. Then, on the third night, he was ambushed and tortured, but still he refused to reveal the whereabouts of the Pearl of the World. Finally, after careful planning, he "skulked like a hunted fox to the beach," removed the pearl from its hiding place and threw it back into the Gulf.

As with other great writers, notably Shakespeare, who took all of his plots or stories from other sources, it is not the source itself that is so important as it is what Steinbeck does with his sources. The above legend is the bare outline, but we should notice all of the significant changes that Steinbeck makes. First, the simplicity of the above parable is made much more complicated in Steinbeck's novel. Instead of having an irresponsible boy who will use the pearl principally for the seduction of young girls and for whimsical prayers for relatives in Purgatory, Steinbeck changes the boy into a father and a husband, a man who sees in the pearl the opportunity to buy an education for his son and thus free him from the bonds that he and his family have always lived under. Furthermore, the other dreams – being married in the church, baptism for their son, new tools to help Kino in his trade, etc., – contrast sharply to the youth in the anecdote.

Whereas the young Indian boy is a simple, flat character, Steinbeck takes the character, gives him a name (Kino) that is based upon a seventeenth-century missionary (who was considered a great man, as the priest points out), and Steinbeck endows him with all of the primitive but human characteristics befitting the hero of a parable such as *The Pearl*. In addition, Steinbeck expands upon his story by the addition of all types of supporting characters—the brother, the priest, the trackers, and, most important, Juana. Steinbeck does, however, retain the pearl buyers, who become forces which are aligned to others with the intent to destroy Kino.

Thus, while Steinbeck begins his story with a simple folk story, he takes the basic situation and, using all sorts of illusions from Western literature, he enriches the basic story and adds various symbolic levels of meaning to it.

THE PEARL: A GENERAL CRITICAL APPROACH

As Steinbeck mentioned in his introduction to this novel, "If this story is a parable, perhaps everyone takes his own meaning from it and reads his own life into it." Likewise, as was noted in the introduction to these Notes, there are many different critical approaches. The following interpretation is only one of many which the novel can support, and it need not be seen as the only definitive approach.

Basically, there are two forces working through the novel—primitive man alone with his labors, toiling close to nature and possessing an innate dignity; and opposing him, man as a predator, as a parasite or a vampire sucking at the vein of life and bringing about death and destruction to the more primitive unit.

The first group is, of course, represented by Kino, his family and his friends who make up the primitive community of fishermen and divers. When we are first introduced to Kino's world, it is warm and content, bathed with the beautiful *Song of the Family*, which gently soothes his heart and makes his life seem fulfilled. Kino and Juana speak very little to each other—it is as though there is no need for words—their communication is innocent and innately understood. In contrast, there is the world of the pearl buyers and the world of the doctor and the priest, representatives of the world with whom Kino and Juana cannot communicate. This is a world which feeds parasitically on these simple people of Kino's village; the doctor's avarice, for example, sends numerous corpses to the church, and the priest is only a puppet of the pearl buyers who are, in turn, only fingers on the arms of some unknown force which has no concern for Kino's class of people.

These two groups are brought together by the use of animal imagery, which Steinbeck uses constantly throughout the novel to comment upon the predatory nature of so-called civilized society. As an illustration, when Coyotito is bitten by the scorpion, the baby's life is in danger, and this horrible, deadly insect makes Kino and Juana realize their ignorance; thus, because of their love for their son, and because of their not knowing about the doctor's fraud, they turn to him for assistance. They believe that because of the doctor, there appears to be a world of possibilities, but in trying to move from one world to another (represented by the long processional, in which the entire village follows Kino and Juana), Kino encounters obstacles which he cannot overcome. For example, Kino suffers mental torture, which is expressed physically when he splits his knuckles battering against the doctor's door in futile rage.

Kino's rage is further expressed when he rows out into the Gulf, and on his first dive, he goes deeper than usual—so deep as to possibly endanger his life; he stays down much longer than usual, but he returns with the Pearl of the World. The animal imagery (or the prey imagery) is now highly functional in relationship to Kino's attitudes. Steinbeck has clearly shown us prior to the discovery of the pearl how the dogs of La Paz feed upon the fish, the larger fish feed upon smaller fish, and every organism depends upon preying upon some other animal. Similarly, as Kino's mind becomes tainted because of his attempted association with the foreign doctor, the pearl also becomes symbolically tainted. When Kino acquires the pearl, it is indeed the most beautiful pearl in the world. But Steinbeck is careful to let us know that this pearl was created through the irritation and the suffering of another organism—the oyster. The beauty of the pearl is not *necessarily* either evil or good. It only becomes either good or evil when Kino and the pearl buyers begin to project their individual desires on it.

When Kino dives for the pearl, his heart is filled with anger and frustration; he is fierce and animal-like in this predatory mood. When he returns to the world above the floor of the Gulf, he is in possession of the Pearl of the World, but the beauty of the pearl slowly begins to dim; it turns ulcerous because Kino's heart changes.

Here, Steinbeck's irony is extremely subtle. On a surface level, it seems that the things which Kino wants are good things: he wants to be married in the church, and he wants Coyotito christened (Juana has been saving the baby's christening clothes until they could find a pearl worthy enough to pay for the occasion), and the ultimate achievement to be wrought by the pearl is an education for Coyotito and a rifle for Kino. On a surface level, it *appears* that Kino wants the right things. But the irony is that Kino and Juana are a truly married couple – they are one as man and wife – they are body and soul. Yet, Kino wants the social recognition of a "foreign marriage" performed by a circumspect priest in a "foreign" religion, and he wants the elegant religious sanction of this foreign religion. (We should remember that earlier, when the scorpion bit Coyotito, Juana first uttered charms in her native religion, and it was only as an afterthought that she added a couple of *Hail Marys*. Furthermore, Kino's new desires are apparently to please members of this new world and its priest rather than his native gods and people. And while it is noble that he wants Coyotito to have an education, the advantages that Kino wants for him lie in the new, foreign world. Kino, still suffering from his recent encounter with the foreign doctor, still wants his son to become a part of the world which has just rejected him.

The ugliness of the new world which Kino so desperately desires to become a part of begins to express itself immediately, but in the same way that Steinbeck shows that the real community is hidden behind paved streets and in gardens that are protected by stone walls, so also the people who attack him are never seen; they remain simply evil forces in the dark. Openly, the doctor comes first with the poisonous white powder which has the power to kill Coyotito; then the priest comes, blessing a marriage that he never performed. But Kino's simple ignorance cannot understand whether or not the doctor has some miraculous knowledge, and thus he yields to the doctor's horrid practice; likewise, the priest represents a similar mysterious religious force. Even though Kino instinctly knows that he is being cheated by the pearl buyers, he clings to the pearl because his very manhood has been challenged by the "dark ones," the unknown ones who attacked him during the night. Kino's predicament is that of any primitive man – his manhood will not allow him to surrender; to complicate matters, Kino has lost one world and has not gained another. In short, Kino is without a society.

As Kino becomes aware of the evil forces trying to rob him of his treasure, he realizes that the pearl has now taken on a different meaning. Earlier, it meant an education for Coyotito and a marriage in the church: now, as Kino and Juana plan their escape, Juana recognizes and Kino acknowledges: "This pearl has become [Kino's] soul." Now Kino is fighting only to prove that he is a man who can protect that which is his. As he becomes like a hunted animal, it is ironic that the reader's sympathy is even more with him *now* than it was earlier. Earlier, Steinbeck used Juana's fears to express the readers' fears. We heard of the attacks from her point of view, and we followed her as she joined Kino in his fight with the "dark ones." But after Steinbeck shows us how Kino's brush house was burned, his canoe destroyed, and how he is being tracked by experts, we sympathize entirely with Kino. For him to relinquish the pearl at this point would not be brave, and at this point, bravery is foremost in Kino's mind.

However, after Coyotito has been killed and after Kino has killed the three trackers, there is nothing left for Kino and Juana to do but to return to town. Yet they do not return in defeat. Counting the three trackers and the man who attacked Kino and was knifed by him, Kino has now killed four men; he has lost his only child, has had his brush house burned and has his canoe destroyed, and yet through it all he has retained his primitive sense of his own manhood and his own worth. The return to the town was Kino's voluntary choice; thus, it is also a moral choice. Kino does not return to accept whatever price that the pearl buyers will offer him, he does not return seeking forgiveness, and he does not return out of fear; Kino's return to town indicates that even though everything that a man possesses, including his beloved son, may be lost, yet man need not be defeated. The throwing of the pearl back into the Gulf, along with his return to the village, comprise Kino's ultimate defiance of a world that refuses to grant him the dignity to which he thought he was entitled. We feel that Kino must know that returning to town could mean his death, but in returning to town, Kino attains a dignity which cannot be stripped from him. Kino's return is not only his defiance of a corrupt world, it is also a simple victory of all that is good in man. As Steinbeck let us know through the animal imagery, in the mountains Kino became an animal; he was tracked and hunted without mercy. In contrast, by returning to his known world, Kino becomes larger than life because *no* force can now defeat him.

As the people watch Kino and Juana pass through the town to the shore of the Gulf, they all recognize this change that has taken place in him; they all recognize Kino's towering strength and his absolute majesty. Juana also recognizes this as she stands proudly beside him and refuses to throw the pearl herself; it is for the newborn man who is still master of his soul to dispose of the pearl as he sees fit.

Therefore, we realize more fully the meaning of Steinbeck's statement "If his story is a parable, perhaps everyone takes his own meaning from it and reads his own life into it." In these lines, Steinbeck sets up no antitheses such as good versus evil, or black versus white. Steinbeck even inverts the major symbol of the pearl. A pearl usually signifies purity and innocence, qualities which a man loses and tries to find. In this novel, Kino possesses innocence and purity at the beginning of the novel, and these simple, beautiful qualities are destroyed after his discovery of the pearl. By inverting the symbolism, Steinbeck emphasizes the parable aspect of his story – that is, we examine what happens to a man when he acquires something so valuable as the Pearl of the World but, after doing so, loses his human dignity and worth in the process. The pearl, then, is a complex symbol – it makes man vulnerable to attacks on his life, but it also makes him stubborn and determined to protect that which is his. Kino and his people have been exploited for four hundred years, and while they fear the foreigners and the unknown, there is also rage and hatred against these intruders. Yet like Kino, they believe that one day they will find the Pearl of the World which will set them free. Thus, if Kino's life is a parable, then it is a parable for many people's own lives: nothing in life is black or white, innocent or evil; everything is a shade somewhere in between. Kino is tricked into seeing and wanting things that are not, in themselves, innately good. He feels that education brings a knowledge that sets a man free. He feels that the church blesses and makes proper husbands and wives. But these things are good only if man is not forced to crawl like an animal to achieve them – that is, a church wedding is not good if one has to lose his manhood to achieve it.

QUESTIONS AND DISCUSSION TOPICS

1. Discuss the various animal imagery that functions throughout the novel: the ants, the scorpion, the hissing snakes, the schools

of fish, the oysters, the dogs, and the pearl buyers as octopuses, etc.

2. Describe in detail Kino and Juana's simple life before and after the discovery of the pearl.

3. How does Steinbeck characterize the doctor? How does he let the reader know that the white powder which the doctor administers to Coyotito is actually a poison which would kill the baby if the doctor did not return?

4. How does the priest function as a travesty of religion?

5. Why are the pearl buyers referred to as "fatherly" and "benevolent"? How does this contradict their real purposes? Are they also victimized?

6. Why are the "dark ones" and the trackers never identified? What is gained by Steinbeck's not identifying them?

7. A symbol can change its meaning during the course of a novel. How does the pearl change its meaning during the course of this novel?

8. Kino believes that it would be better to kill a person than to kill a canoe because a canoe has no relatives to revenge it. What types of values are operative in such a statement?

9. Kino and Juana function more or less on a primitive level in their lives and in their religion, yet they both want a church wedding and a christening for Coyotito. How are these values consistent with their lives? How are they contradictory?

10. What is the function of the many "songs" that Kino hears during the course of the novel?

SELECTED BIBLIOGRAPHY

STEINBECK'S CHIEF WORKS
Fiction

Cup of Gold. New York: Robert M. McBride & Co., 1929.

The Pastures of Heaven. New York: Brewer, Warren & Putnam, 1932.

To a God Unknown. New York: Robert O. Ballou, 1933.

Tortilla Flat. New York: Covici-Friede, 1935.

In Dubious Battle. New York: Covici-Friede, 1936.

The Red Pony. New York: Covici-Friede, 1937; The Viking Press, 1945. (Included in *The Long Valley*, 1938).

Of Mice and Men. New York: Covici-Friede, 1937.

The Long Valley. New York: The Viking Press, 1938.

The Grapes of Wrath. New York: The Viking Press, 1939.

The Moon Is Down. New York: The Viking Press, 1942.

Cannery Row. New York: The Viking Press, 1945.

The Wayward Bus. New York: The Viking Press, 1947.

The Pearl. New York: The Viking Press, 1947.

Burning Bright. New York: The Viking Press, 1950.

East of Eden. New York: The Viking Press, 1952.

Sweet Thursday. New York: The Viking Press, 1954.

The Short Reign of Pippin IV: A Fabrication. New York: The Viking Press, 1957.

The Winter of Our Discontent. New York: The Viking Press, 1961.

Nonfiction

Sea of Cortez: A Leisurely Journal of Travel and Research (in collaboration with Edward F. Ricketts). New York: The Viking Press, 1941.

Bombs Away: The Story of a Bomber Team. New York: The Viking Press, 1942.

A Russian Journal. New York: The Viking Press, 1948.

The Log from the Sea of Cortez. New York: The Viking Press, 1951.

Once There Was a War. New York: The Viking Press, 1958.

Travels with Charley in Search of America. New York: The Viking Press, 1962.

CRITICAL AND INTERPRETATIVE STUDIES

Fontenrose, Joseph. *John Steinbeck: An Introduction and Interpretation.* New York: Barnes and Noble, 1963.

Lisca, Peter. *The Wide World of John Steinbeck.* New Brunswick: Rutgers University Press, 1958.

Moore, Harry Thornton. *The Novels of John Steinbeck: A First Critical Study.* Chicago: Normandie House, 1939.

Tedlock. E. W., Jr., and Wicker, C. V., editors. *Steinbeck and His Critics: A Record of Twenty-Five Years.* Albuquerque: University of New Mexico Press, 1957.

Watt, F. W. *John Steinbeck.* New York: Grove Press; Edinburgh: Oliver and Boyd; 1962.